In
CLASSICAL
mood

Tranquilit

Tranquility

 n a world that seems to spin ever faster, few pleasures can be so instantly relied upon to invoke a calm and serene state of mind as listening to classical music. This volume of *In Classical Mood* has thirteen of the most tranquil pieces ever written, from Mozart's sublime *Clarinet Concerto* and Beethoven's enduringly popular *Für Elise*, to Fauré's melancholy *Pavane* and the Spanish composer Rodrigo's courtly guitar classic *Fantasia para un Gentilhombre*. So sit back, listen, and relax. You've earned it.

THE LISTENER'S GUIDE — WHAT THE SYMBOLS MEAN

THE COMPOSERS
Their lives... their loves.. their legacies...

THE MUSIC
Explanation... analysis... interpretation...

THE INSPIRATION
How works of genius came to be written

THE BACKGROUND
People, places, and events linked to the music

© MCMXCVI IMP AB In Classical Mood™ IMP AB, produced under license by IMP Inc. Printed in China. US P 2201 12 003

Contents

EDVARD GRIEG *1843–1907*

Peer Gynt Suite No. 1

PRELUDE (MORNING)

A famous piece of incidental music from the play *Peer Gynt*, "Morning" is a masterly evocation of this time of day. From the first tentative calls on the flute to the soft and gently flowing main melody, few of Edvard Grieg's compositions evoke such a sublime feeling of peace and tranquility in the listener.

COMPOSER MEETS DRAMATIST

It was in 1874 that Norway's greatest dramatist, Henrik Ibsen, asked Norway's greatest composer, Grieg, to write some incidental music to accompany his play *Peer Gynt*. Grieg hesitated, doubting whether his own lyrical musical style was at all suited to the colorful, action-packed nature of Ibsen's play. Indeed, composing the music cost Grieg much anxiety and effort, but it also proved to be some of his finest and best-loved work.

THE STORY OF PEER GYNT

Peer Gynt is different from Ibsen's other plays, which deal with serious social and political issues of the day. This is a fantasy, in which the youthful hero of the title roams far and wide, getting involved in one adventure after another. He later returns home, an older and wiser man, to Norway and to his faithful sweetheart, Solveig. At a more profound level, the play is about "learning by experience" and is a comment on what Ibsen believed were mankind's strengths and weaknesses.

Left: *The celebrated dramatist Ibsen.*

The Norwegian actor Bjoern Bjoernson (right) in an 1892 production of Peer Gynt *at the Christiania Theater in Oslo.*

A poster by Norwegian artist Edvard Munch (left) for an 1896 production in Paris.

FOLLOWING SUITES

Grieg made up two suites (groups of pieces) from his incidental music to *Peer Gynt* especially for concert performance. Among the other tunes in these suites are such well-known and popular pieces as "In the Hall of the Mountain King," "Arabian Dance," "Anitra's Dance," and the hauntingly beautiful "Solveig's Song."

KEY NOTES

Fellow Norwegian Harald Severud followed in Grieg's footsteps by writing music for Peer Gynt, along with a pair of orchestral suites.

CLAUDE DEBUSSY
1862–1918

Arabesque No.1

Claude Debussy's intent with *Arabesque No.1* was to create a light, florid piece rather than one with deep emotional appeal. Like the delicate, decorative pattern from which it derives its name, this charming piece of piano music is as ornamental as a spider's web.

A NEW KIND OF COMPOSER

In addition to being an admired pianist, Claude Debussy is thought to be one of France's finest composers. He wrote for the piano as no one before him had ever dreamed of: Sometimes the notes were bunched together, while other times they were placed at the ends of the keyboard; and pedals were used to make notes and harmonies shift and blend. The result was a new and magical world of sound that inspired several generations of classical and jazz musicians.

AN INDEPENDENT TALENT

The French composer Claude Debussy was a brilliant student at the Paris Conservatoire de Musique, where he won the highest prizes for composition. He was also a rebel and would often alarm his professors by sitting at the piano and playing chords that broke every textbook rule. What he was beginning to do was search for a new musical language, and slowly but surely he found it. He also found inspiration in the same images as those that attracted the French Impressionist painters—clouds, rain, wind, water, sunlight, and shadow. It all helped to make Debussy one of the most original composers of modern times.

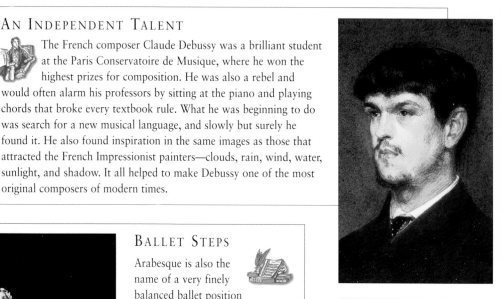

BALLET STEPS

Arabesque is also the name of a very finely balanced ballet position in which the weight of the body is on one leg, while the other leg is extended behind. Similarly, one arm is stretched out in front, while the other arm reaches back. And just as Debussy's *Arabesque* is enchanting to listen to, this precise and graceful ballet move is most beautiful to watch. Today, there are many subtle variations on the basic position *(left)*.

KEY NOTES

During his summer vacations, the young Debussy was much in demand as a pianist at fashionable gatherings. Eventually his name reached the ears of the Russian socialite Madame Nadezhda von Meck, patron of Tchaikovsky, and the talented rebel joined her musical circle for a while.

SIR EDWARD ELGAR *1857–1934*

Serenade for Strings in E Minor

OPUS 20: SECOND MOVEMENT

The young Edward Elgar was fond of the soft, warm tones created by the stringed instruments of the orchestra. For this exquisite serenade, he composed long, flowing lines of melody to convey a tender mood that is accented by a hint of deeper passion and melancholy. It can be compared to a painting in sound of the English landscape that Elgar loved.

STRUGGLING TO MAKE HIS NAME

Elgar was thirty-five years old when he wrote *Serenade for Strings*, yet he was still struggling to make his name. Born in the heart of rural England, Elgar worked in a lawyer's office before deciding on music as a career. He mostly taught himself composition, while giving violin lessons and playing the church organ. But even with his wife Alice's support, he still had to wait until he was over forty before he made his mark in the world.

THE ENGLISH GENTLEMAN

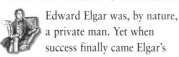

Edward Elgar was, by nature, a private man. Yet when success finally came Elgar's way, he suddenly found himself built up to be a national hero. Obligingly, he wrote some magnificent symphonies, concertos, and marches to echo the pageantry of the British Empire, which was then at its height. He was happy to play the role expected of him—that of a grand and dignified English gentleman—but there always remained a part of him that craved the peace and solitude found in *Serenade for Strings*.

PASSING THE TIME

As a young man, Elgar enjoyed many pastimes, including chemistry, which he explored in his home laboratory *(above)*. He also practiced various sporting activities, such as golf and kite-flying. After the death of his wife and as he grew older, his interests changed to less energetic ones, such as his pet dogs and horse racing.

KEY NOTES

The String Quartet *and* Introduction and Allegro for String Orchestra *are two more of the famous shorter works by Elgar that were inspired by his great love of stringed instruments.*

MODEST MUSSORGSKY *1839–1881 (ORCHESTRATED BY MAURICE RAVEL)*

Pictures at an Exhibition

THE OLD CASTLE

To a quiet accompaniment on the strings, first the bassoon and then the saxophone share a peaceful, but also rather wistful, tune. It is inspired by the picture of an old, half-ruined castle and the figure of a troubadour writing poetry and playing music within its walls. The musical imagery of Modest Mussorgsky and his orchestrator, Maurice Ravel, conveys a mood of romantic nostalgia for an age long departed.

A POSTHUMOUS EXHIBITION

Pictures at an Exhibition is a masterpiece of the scene-setting type of music known as "program" music. It was inspired by a posthumous exhibition of ten paintings and drawings by an artist friend of Mussorgsky named Victor Hartman *(left)*. The whole set of colorfully descriptive pieces is given unity by a grand and dignified theme called "Promenade," which is heard at the beginning and then repeated through the piece as the visitor to the exhibition strolls from picture to picture.

RAVEL'S ORCHESTRATION

Mussorgsky wrote *Pictures at an Exhibition* for the piano, but fellow composer Nikolai Andreyevich Rimsky-Korsakoff, who edited most of Mussorgsky's posthumous

publications, didn't believe it could be orchestrated. Even so, the originality and power of the music have prompted several musicians to do so, such as the French composer Ravel *(left)*. His use of the saxophone in "The Old Castle" is just one of Ravel's typically brilliant instrumental effects.

STOP THE CLOCK

One wild and furious piece in *Pictures at an Exhibition* is called "Baba-yaga" or "Hut on Fowl's Legs." It was named after a wicked and terrifying witch from Russian legend who lives in a ramshackle hut, which is supported on giant chicken's legs. Mussorgsky's inspiration came from Victor Hartman's fantastic design for a clock *(right)*.

DASHING YOUNG MAN

Russian composer Modest Mussorgsky began his adult life as an army officer. Then he met fellow Russian composer Mily Balakirev, who fired his enthusiasm for music. After resigning his army commission, Mussorgsky joined the small group of fellow Russian composers known as "The Five," and with them began writing music with a strong Russian sound and feel to it.

He was especially interested in echoing the inflections of Russian speech in his music. *Pictures at an Exhibition* dates from 1874, when Mussorgsky was still only thirty-five. In addition to this sublime piece, he was responsible for some remarkable songs, as well as his great opera, *Boris Godunov*, which was based on episodes from Russian history.

A SAD ENDING

The great tragedy of Mussorgsky's life is that such a promising musical talent probably never reached his full potential. He began drinking heavily in his thirties and soon became an alcoholic. He eventually died as a result of alcoholism at age of forty-two, with several important commissions left unfinished. In this famous portrait of Mussorgsky *(right)*

by Russian artist Ilya Repin, painted a few days before the composer's death, the damage that Mussorgsky's lifestyle inflicted on him is evident.

KEY NOTES

Mussorgsky's most famous song is The Song of the Flea, *a musical setting of words by the great German poet and dramatist Goethe.*

FREDERICK DELIUS *1862–1934*

Florida Suite

BY THE RIVER

fter a few rippling bars on solo flute, the violins embark on a long, leisurely melody, suggesting the lazy motion of Lake Okeechobee, the gateway to the Everglades. In his portrait of the flow of this body of water, the English composer Frederick Delius conjures up the perfect remedy for a distracted mind.

IN PARADISE

In 1884 the young Delius moved to Solano Grove near Jacksonville, Florida to manage an orange grove. Neglecting his oranges, Delius instead concentrated on his music. The beauty of the luxuriant surroundings, coupled with the song and dance of the local populations, inspired this early *Florida Suite*.

KEY NOTES

Another of Delius's works, also inspired by his time in the States is Appalachia, *for baritone voice, chorus, and orchestra.*

WOLFGANG AMADEUS
MOZART *1756–1791*

Clarinet Concerto

SECOND MOVEMENT

Written for what was one of his favorite instruments, this haunting piece was completed on September 28, 1791, shortly before Wolfgang Amadeus Mozart's death. This was the last concerto the great composer ever wrote. It is surprising that in its sublime serenity, there is no hint of the turbulence that is supposed to have marked his later years.

MAN OF MANY CONCERTOS

Mozart wrote concertos for almost every instrument of his time. Heading the list are his twenty-nine piano concertos. Then there are his concertos for violin, violin and viola, horn, clarinet, bassoon, oboe, and flute, (and for instruments in various combinations), plus the enduring *Concerto for Flute and Harp*.

KEY NOTES

This concerto movement is marked andantino, which means "little andante," or to be taken at a very leisurely pace.

JOHANN SEBASTIAN BACH
1685–1750

Cantata

BMV 208, "WHERE SHEEP MAY SAFELY GRAZE"

*I*mages of pastoral tranquility and peace inspired Bach to write this cantata. Considered one of his most serene melodies, it is popularly known in English-speaking countries as *Where Sheep May Safely Graze*. It is one of the 15 numbers from *Was mir behagt, ist nur die muntre Jagd ("The merry chase, the hunt is my delight")*, which introduces four mythological characters: The heavenly huntress Diana, the eager hunter Endymion, and the pastoral gods Pan and Pales. *Where Sheep May Safely Graze* is the charming aria of Pales for two recorders and a soprano. It is considered one of the most intimate pastorals Bach ever wrote.

THE CANTATA

The *cantata* (from the Italian *cantare*, "to sing") is simply a composition for voices and instruments. Cantatas were particularly popular in the Baroque period of the 17th and early 18th centuries. Bach wrote hundreds of cantatas, both religious and secular (non-religious).

13

A MUSICAL FAMILY

The German Bach family represents the most famous dynasty in musical history. For more than 300 years—from the 16th into the 18th century—members of the family were active in just about every branch of music. In some parts of Germany, the very name "Bach" was synonymous with "musician." Johann Sebastian's father, Johann Ambrosius, was a fine violinist and organist; two of J.S. Bach's sons, Carl Philipp Emanuel and Johann Christian, were famous composers.

Bach (above, left) with Gottfried Heinrich, the first son of his second marriage, and the two elder sons of his first marriage, Carl Philipp Emanuel and Wilhelm Friedemann.

RELIGIOUS CANTATAS

Bach wrote many religious *cantatas* while he was cantor (director of music) at the St. Thomaskirche *(left)* in Leipzig, from 1723 until his death in 1750. His punishing work schedule meant that he had to write a fresh *cantata*—and rehearse it thoroughly with the choir—in time for each new Sunday service.

KEY NOTES

Where Sheep May Safely Graze is *the best known of Bach's secular cantatas. Another one is known as the* Coffee Cantata, *which celebrates the pleasures of coffee drinking, a fashionable 18th-century pastime.*

GABRIEL FAURÉ *1845–1924*

Pavane

OPUS 50

Gabriel Fauré completed *Pavane*, a lovely arrangement for a string orchestra, in 1887. In this much-loved piece, violins and violas divide the melody between them—like dancers moving slowly through a solemn ritual—while cellos and double basses provide a soft, steady *pizzicato* (plucked) background accompaniment. This courtly music breathes an air of measured tranquility that is all its own.

A POPULAR DANCE

The *pavan* ("pavane" in French) is a stately dance that originated in Renaissance Italy. It soon became popular in the royal courts of Europe, including that of Queen Elizabeth I, where it was often paired with a livelier dance called the *galliard*. In Spain, the pavan was danced at times of mourning, giving it the solemn character that later attracted composers such as Fauré.

KEY NOTES

Fauré's Pavane exists in several versions. One features the flute and other woodwind instruments; another brings in a large choir.

JOAQUIN RODRIGO *1901–*

Fantasia para un Gentilhombre

(FOR GUITAR AND ORCHESTRA): FIRST MOVEMENT

Old-world gallantry is as much a part of Spain as the drama of the bullfight. This courtly and dignified aspect of the Spanish character is what Joaquin Rodrigo portrays in his aptly titled *Fantasia para un Gentilhombre* ("Fantasy for a Gentleman"), which he dedicated to his friend André Segovia. It includes a gentle dialogue between orchestra and solo guitar, with the melody shifting from one to the other in the manner of a stately dance. Such music belongs to a world where there is time enough for the courtesies of life.

THE CLASSICAL GUITAR

The guitar was probably first introduced to Spain by the Moors of north Africa, who occupied the country during the Middle Ages. But it was the 19th-century Spanish guitar maker Antonio de Torres Jurado who developed the six-string classical guitar *(left)* as an orchestral instrument, and the composer Francisco Tárrega (1852–1909) who pioneered the playing techniques to go with it.

FOR SEGOVIA

Rodrigo dedicated *Fantasia para un Gentilhombre* to the Spanish guitarist Andrés Segovia *(right)*, who was born near Granada in 1894 and died in Madrid in 1987.

AGAINST THE ODDS

The Spanish composer Rodrigo was blind from age 3. This did not stop him from composing—he had the help of a special braille composing machine—nor from becoming Professor of Music History at Madrid

University. As a composer, Rodrigo loved the guitar above all other instruments, and many of his works, including *Fantasia para un Gentilhombre*, are for guitar and orchestra. Most famous of these pieces is his *Concierto de Aranjuez*, written during the Spanish Civil War.

KEY NOTES

Some scholars believe that the name of the guitar may be derived from an ancient Greek stringed instrument called the kithara.

ORPHEUS AND EURYDICE: DANCE OF THE BLESSED SPIRITS

CHRISTOPH WILLIBALD GLUCK *1714–1787*

Orpheus and Eurydice

DANCE OF THE BLESSED SPIRITS

This is a musical evocation of *Elysium*, or the Elysian Fields, the ancient Greek idea of heaven where "blessed" spirits dance in peace. Flute and strings perform a graceful duet, the music switching from one section to another and back again. With the warm, delicate tones of the flute, the silky backdrop of the strings, and the music's measured, untroubled pace, Christoph Willibald Gluck simply but magically creates his own picture of celestial serenity.

GREEK MYTHOLOGY

The story of Orpheus and Eurydice is from Greek mythology. Orpheus is permitted to go down to Hades (the Underworld) in search of his dead wife, Eurydice. He may return with her to earthly life, provided that he does not look back at her on the way. However, he cannot resist one backward glance, therefore losing her again. In Gluck's opera, Orpheus is forgiven and there is a happy ending. The "Dance of the Blessed Spirits" comes after Orpheus has charmed the Furies (demons) with his singing and has entered Elysium.

A KEY FIGURE IN OPERA

A German-born composer, Gluck is one of the key figures in opera. He settled in Vienna, where he was head of opera at the Court Theater, then moved to Paris, which at the time was an even more influential center. His operas are based mostly on Greek mythology or ancient history.

HIGH VOICES

The part of Orpheus was originally written for a *castrato*—a boy castrated so that his voice did not break. Castrati, such as the great Farinelli (1705–1782) *(right)*, were among the highest paid stars of their day. Today, roles such as these, including Gluck's "Orpheus," are usually sung not by a man, but by a woman who has a deep, rich voice called a *contralto*.

KEY NOTES

The most famous aria in this opera is Orpheus's lament, "Che farò senza Euridice?" ("What shall I do without Eurydice?") when he thinks he's lost his wife for the second time.

JULES MASSENET
1842–1912

Thaïs

MÉDITATION

editation helps induce a calmer, more tranquil state of mind. In this piece, it is invoked by the soft tones of solo violin and the delicate, mournful notes of the harp. In the opera from which it comes, this particular "Méditation" brings about a change of heart, from a sinful way of life to a spiritual one.

A DRAMATIC LINK

Jules Massenet's celebrated "Méditation" is, technically, an *intermezzo*. This Italian word means "between" or "in the middle of." As used in many operas, it is a piece of orchestral music placed between two scenes to provide a dramatic link from one to the other. Occasionally, composers have used the term *intermezzo* more loosely to describe any fairly brief orchestral or instrumental piece.

HIGHEST HONORS

 Massenet was one of the most successful composers of French opera, combining exotic drama with seductive melodies, of which *Thaïs* is a fine example. In Paris he was also a leader of the fashionable musical society and, as a student, won highest honors at the Paris Conservatoire de Musique, returning there later as a distinguished professor.

TESTS OF FAITH

The opera *Thaïs* is set in Egypt in the early days of Christianity. Thaïs is a beautiful dancer and courtesan (paid escort). A Christian monk Athanaël converts her to his faith, but cannot help falling in love with her. Later, Thaïs dies, happy in her belief in a heavenly afterlife. Meanwhile Athanaël, first suffers the torments of desire for her and

Left: *A poster for* Thaïs *from 1894.*

then of grief after her death.

KEY NOTES

Massenet's best-known opera, Manon, *is also about the rescue and reform of a courtesan, although in this case, Manon dies miserably. Manon was first performed at the Opéra-Comique in Paris in 1884, establishing Massenet's position as the most popular opera composer of his day.*

21

LUDWIG VAN BEETHOVEN *1770–1827*

Bagatelle in A Minor

"FÜR ELISE"

E ven Beethoven, the most dynamic and dramatic of composers, had his moments of relaxing music. The relative simplicity of this famous piano piece is a large part of its charm. With *Für Elise*, he strove to express feelings of love and affection and, in the process, penned a melody that has soothed the minds and spirits of millions.

FEMININE CHARMS

Beethoven never married, though he had many female admirers. Among those to whom he lost his heart were: Bettina Brentano; the Countesses von Brunsvik, Therese and Josephine; the Countess Giulietta Guicciardi *(above)*; Therese Malfatti. There was also a letter found after his death, to a mysterious "Immortal Beloved." As for the "Elise" of this piece, some scholars believe that his publisher misread his dedication and "Elise" was really "Therese."

KEY NOTES

Beethoven wrote a number of fairly short piano pieces, such as Für Elise, which are called bagatelles, or trifles.

ANTONIN DVOŘÁK *1841–1904*

Symphony No. 9 in E Minor

OPUS 95, "FROM THE NEW WORLD": SECOND MOVEMENT

Rather dark and somber chords on the brass instruments of the orchestra quickly give way to a broad and idyllic melody, played on the *cor anglais* (an alto oboe) to a hushed background of strings.

There are moments of restlessness, liveliness, and excitement later in the movement, before the lovely cor anglais melody returns, impressing on our minds the welcome peace of a calm and golden landscape.

THE NEW WORLD

Antonin Dvořák traveled to the U.S. in 1892, at the invitation of a rich patron of the arts, Mrs. Jeanette Thurber, to become director of her conservatory of music in New York. He was quickly inspired by the music of the "New World," especially the songs of Native Americans and of African Americans. Dvořák combined these rhythms with folk tunes of his country—you can find an echo of these sounds in much of the music he composed during his three years in America.

FAMILY CONCERNS

Dvořák was a devoted family man *(above)*. Tragically, he and his wife, Anna, lost their first three children in infancy. But with their remaining six children, they formed the happiest of families. One of their daughters married Dvořák's star pupil, the Czech composer Josef Suk. Aside from his family, Dvořák's special interests included railroad trains and pigeons—he was deeply upset when one day someone served him pigeon pie!

From Bohemia to New York

Known as the most celebrated composer of what is now Czechoslovakia, Antonin Dvořák grew up in a village in old Bohemia where his father was the innkeeper and local butcher. From infancy, Dvořák was surrounded by musicians, and he went on to study music in the Bohemian capital, Prague. But for years, life was hard as he struggled to make his name. It was support from the great German composer Brahms that finally helped Dvořák gain international recognition. Famous at last, mainly through his melodic symphonies and lively slavonic dances, he made two triumphant extended tours of the U.S. and remained Director of the National Conservatory in New York until 1894.

He spent his holidays in America in Spillville, Iowa (below), a remote township of Czech immigrants.

English Horn

The French-named *cor anglais*, which features so prominently in the slow movement of the "New World" symphony, is a woodwind instrument. It is similar to an oboe, but with deeper notes and a richer sound. The name, which means "English horn," is rather odd, since the *cor anglais* is neither particularly English, nor is it any kind of a horn!

KEY NOTES

Dvořák said of America: "This country is full of melody, original, sympathetic, and varying in mood, color, and character to suit every phase of composition."

Credits & Acknowledgments

PICTURE CREDITS

Cover /Title and Contents Pages/ IBC: Images Colour Library

AKG London: 3(l & c), 5(r), 9(bl), 14(b), 16, 19(bl); Jorg P. Anders: 14(t); Beethoven-Haus, Bonn: 22; Bridgeman Art Library, London/Guildford Borough Council: 6; Tretyakov Gallery, Moscow: 10(r); City of Bristol Museum & Art Gallery: 18-19; National Museum of American Art, Smithsonian Institution: 23; Corbis-Bettmann: 24(l & bl); David Muench: 11; The Elgar Foundation: 7(r); Eye Ubiquitous/Mike Southern: 17(tl); Fine Art Photographic Library: 15, 20; Robert Harding Picture Library: 4; Images Colour Library: 2, 13; Lebrecht Collection: 3(r), 7(l), 10(l), 17(bc), 19(r), 24(tl & tr), 25(l); Morris: 21(l); MC Picture Library/Chris Barker: 17tr; Brian Delf: 25(r); Novosti Photo Library: 9(t & br); Performing Arts Library/ Linda Rich: 5(l); Roger-Viollet: 21(r); Woodfall Wild Images/Jeremy Moore: 8; Ted Mead: 12.

All illustrations and symbols: John See